Ahoy!

A pirate goes to

see!

Alexandra Spichtig

Illustrated by Antonella Fant

Published by Miriam Laundry Publishing Company
www.miriamlaundry.com

Photo of Alexandra Spichtig by Kristy Dooley
Photo of Antonella Fant by Dario Andres Tiscornia

Essex Junction, Vermont
Library of Congress Control Number: 2023917036

HC ISBN 978-1-77944-006-8
PB ISBN 978-1-77944-005-1
e-Book ISBN 978-1-77944-004-4

Written by Alexandra Spichtig
www.alexandraspichtig.com
Illustrated and Designed by Antonella Fant
www.antonellafant.com

To all the children who doubt their genius and potential because they struggle with reading.

Max is sitting in his 2nd-grade classroom. He is looking out the window. He is thinking about his best friend, Coco. Max is remembering all the pirate adventures they've had together.

Coco is a parrot. But she is not a *real* parrot. She is a *robot* parrot. Coco was a present from Max's older sister, Gina. "Every smart pirate needs a parrot!" she said.

Gina was right. With Coco by his side, Max feels like a real pirate. In his favorite outfit, he looks like a pirate. He even talks like a pirate. Coco understands when Max says,

"Ahoy matey! Arrgh! Yo ho ho!"

"Max, are you daydreaming again?" Ms. Miller, his teacher, calls from the front of the class.

Max used to think that school was fun. He also used to think that he was smart. But he does not think that anymore. The longer Max is in school, the less he likes it. Max does not feel smart anymore.

The school bell rings. Max will need to finish his schoolwork at home, **again!**

When Max gets home, he races to his bedroom.

"Ahoy, Coco! Weigh anchor!"

"AYE, AYE, CAPTAIN!"

Coco replies.

Together, Max and Coco defend their bedroom from bandits. Most pirates are known for stealing, but Max is a different kind of pirate. Max likes helping people.

9

Max and Coco jump when Gina bursts into the bedroom.
"Max, quick! To the galley! Mom wants the whole crew at the
dinner table! Now!"

10

After dinner, Dad asks, "Did you do your homework, Max?"

"Oops! I forgot," Max says. "I need to finish a worksheet."

"What about your daily reading?" Mom asks.

"Not yet," Max mumbles.

"You have not done either one?" Mom is not happy with him, Max can tell.

Reading is hard for Max. He loses his place over and over. He skips words, even though he doesn't mean to. Sometimes Max guesses words he doesn't know.

"Max, are you even trying?"
Dad sounds frustrated.

"I am trying!" Max answers.
"I try to chase the words and
read them before they move."

Dad frowns.
"Don't make up stories."

Max bursts into tears.
"I'm not! I'm telling
the truth!"

"Tell me again what you see, Max," Mom asks.

"The words move on the page," Max explains.
"Sometimes they stick together. Sometimes they hide behind each other. Sometimes they pull apart."

He takes a deep breath. "Sometimes there is a shadow around letters. Sometimes words are like water. Letters dance like waves. They move up and down. I have to chase them."

Mom and Dad look at each other.

"It's so hard!"

Max cries. "The harder I try, the more it hurts my eyes and head."

"OK, Max," Mom says. "Time for bed. Let's give your eyes and head a rest tonight."

The next day, Mom takes Max to a vision specialist so he can check Max's eyes.

"Hello, Max. I hear that reading is giving you some trouble," says Dr. Costa. "Let's take a look and figure out what is going on."

After Dr. Costa is done with the exam, he says, "I have good news for you, Max. Your eyes are healthy. Your eyesight is fine. But...

...the reason you see shadows and dancing letters is because your eyes don't work well as a team," Dr. Costa adds.

Max is quiet for a moment as he figures this out.
"My eyes need to work together like a good pirate crew works together on a ship."

"That's right, Max! To help your eyes learn how to work better as a team, I want you to do some vision exercises."

"Vision exercises?" Max grumbles.

"Pirates don't do that!"

Dr. Costa chuckles. "A pirate needs very good visual skills, Max. If a pirate is on a stormy sea, he needs to be able to keep his balance while he guides his ship. Try this. Stand on one foot. Track my moving pen with your eyes."

"This is hard," Max groans as he wobbles.

Bracing Max, Dr. Costa explains, "If you do these exercises, you will feel steadier. You will no longer have to chase words. Reading will become much easier. You will be able to read treasure maps more quickly too, Max."

Max crosses his arms over his chest. He isn't convinced.

"Will this help?" Dr. Costa holds up an eye patch. "For some activities, you will wear one of these."

Max grins and puts on the eye patch.

"Aye, aye, Matey!"

Every day after school, Max and Coco work together. Gina is their coach. They do many different activities.

Sometimes Max gets to wear the eye patch so he can train one eye at a time.

With other exercises, Max and Coco lie on the floor while Gina moves around pirate treasures above their heads. They have to follow the treasure only with their eyes without moving their heads.

One activity is like doing magic. Max has to turn two pictures into one by looking at a point in front of the pictures. Looking at the tip of a pencil makes this easy.

Spy training is especially fun. Max feels like he is on a pirate mission. Gina draws or writes fun things on cards and spreads them all around the room. Some are close, some are farther away. Max has to look at each card without leaving his watch post and tell Gina what he sees.

After a few weeks of practice, Max can see things more clearly and much faster.

It is time for Max to visit Dr. Costa again.

"Great job, Max! Your eyes are working much better as a team."

Max smiles. "My eyes and head no longer hurt. I no longer have to chase words." He proudly adds, "And best of all, I now finish my work at school!"

Back home, Max races to his bedroom. He is happy he doesn't have any schoolwork to finish. Now he has lots of time to read books. Tonight, he is reading *How to Train a Pirate Parrot*.

Max orders. "Ahoy, Coco! Weigh anchor!"

It is time for your training."

"AYE, AYE, CAPTAIN!"

Max loves to read with Coco. They learn lots of fun things.

Max feels like the smartest pirate ever!

FOUR TYPES OF VISUAL SKILLS ACTIVITIES MAX DID

Scan this code to download resources, including directions for a DIY pirate eye patch!

https://alexandraspichtig.com/books

WHY ARE THESE ACTIVITIES IMPORTANT?

Walk the Plank (visual attention & fixation flexibility)

This activity helps the eyes develop the ability to focus quickly after shifting their gaze from one location to another. Being able to shift your gaze accurately and effortlessly is an important skill required to easily orient yourself within any given environment. This is especially important to become fluent in reading as it helps you navigate lines of text and fixate on words efficiently, so you can enjoy what you read rather than feel exhausted by the process of reading.

Follow the Target (tracking & eye-movement control)

This activity helps develop the ability to easily and smoothly pursue targets with the eyes only, without moving the head, even when targets cross the midline of the body. Effective eye-movement control is an important skill required to be able to efficiently navigate lines of print while reading and doing other tasks that depend on precise and fluid eye movements.

Flat Fusion Cards (binocular fusion & eye teaming)

This activity helps develop a flexible interaction between the focusing and eye-teaming systems. Effective binocular fusion and eye-teaming skills help you see crisp sharp images. These skills are also the basis for good depth perception because your brain combines the images it receives from each eye separately to create a single 3D image.

Spying (accommodation)

This activity helps the eyes develop the ability to effectively and efficiently shift focus between different locations, including locations at different distances. This skill allows you to efficiently shift focus back and forth between near-vision tasks (e.g., reading, doing worksheets, or catching a ball) and far-vision tasks (e.g., looking at a smartboard or chalkboard, reading signs, or aiming a ball).

NOTE FROM THE AUTHOR

Many children with visual skill gaps do not realize that how they see does not match how everybody else sees. Their eyes look healthy. Consequently, the source of their struggles often goes overlooked. This story is intended to raise awareness regarding how important visual skills are for effective learning.

Over the course of several decades, as a classroom teacher, instructional designer, and researcher, I have seen the light of enthusiastic, curious students start to dim as self-doubt begins to creep in, causing them to believe that they are struggling with reading because they are not smart enough. Yet the children and the adults in their lives did not realize that some of them were struggling because they had not yet developed the visual skills necessary to learn to read efficiently.

Visual skills are foundational to students' academic readiness. More than a dozen visual skills are required to efficiently engage with learning tasks. In fact, it is estimated that over 70% of typical classroom activities involve visual skills in some fashion. Signs of visual skill issues include a short attention span, fatiguing quickly, and being easily distracted. Children with visual skill gaps often have a very labored reading process. They do not like to read and avoid it whenever possible, often claiming they do not like to read because it is boring. When reading, they may lose their place frequently, often repeating or skipping words or lines. They may confuse similar words or fail to recognize the same words in the next sentence. They may be unable to visualize what is read. Some may tilt their head while reading. They may complain about headaches or eye strain. To them, words may appear to move on the page as they read.

Both people with great eyesight and people with glasses can have visual skill gaps. The good news is that research has shown that visual skills are developmental and can be improved through targeted exercises. Just like we develop skills in sports through practice, we can develop our visual skills for reading and learning. An added benefit is that kids who develop their visual skills often experience improved athletic performance too! Before questioning struggling students' efforts or their cognitive capabilities, it is advisable to confirm that students have developed the necessary visual skills. Visual skill examples include tracking (eyes moving accurately, smoothly, and quickly from place to place), binocular coordination (both eyes working together as a team), accommodation (the ability to quickly shift focus between near and distant targets), and visual processing (the ability to understand what we are looking at).

My hope is that this story can be a conversation starter, providing children with language to help them describe what they see and helping adults to notice signs and know what questions to ask. Naturally, depending on the severity of their visual skill gaps, some children, like Max, may benefit from a professional screening by a behavioral/developmental optometrist. The College of Optometry and Vision Development website (www.covd.org) provides many wonderful resources, including a *Quality of Life Survey* to determine the need for a professional screening along with a list of recommended specialists in your area. The Optometric Extension Program Foundation's website (www.oepf.org) is another helpful resource for finding a behavioral/developmental optometrist near you.

As a final note, while this book focuses on visual skills, similar care and consideration needs to be given to children's auditory processing and motor skills, as deficits in these areas can also impact learning.

ABOUT THE AUTHOR

Alexandra (Alex) Spichtig has dedicated her career to education and researching and understanding the role of eye movements and visual skills in reading. She began her career as a classroom teacher in Switzerland before moving to the U.S., where she earned a Master's Degree in Teaching English as a Second or Foreign Language, and her Ph.D. in Instructional Design for Online Learning. In her former role as Chief Research Officer at Reading Plus, Alex incorporated her groundbreaking research on silent reading proficiency into instructional and assessment tools focused on developing students' silent-reading proficiency and measuring unique aspects of reading including comprehension-based silent reading rate and motivation for reading.

Alex has presented at various international conferences related to literacy and eye-movement research and co-authored book chapters and peer-reviewed journal articles. Among them was a landmark study that analyzed changes in silent reading efficiency over a 50-year span, published in Reading Research Quarterly in 2016.

In her current role as cofounder and CEO of the Stanford Taylor Foundation, Alex leads research efforts focused on visual skill development and the relationship between visual skill proficiency and academic success. Alex is committed to promoting a broader understanding of the essential role visual and perceptual skills play in reading, learning, and sports.

ABOUT THE ILLUSTRATOR

Maria Antonella Fant was born, and currently lives, in Argentina. She is a visual designer, a children's book illustrator, and a concept artist, having studied Graphic Design and Illustration. From a very young age, Antonella has been self-driven. As she grew up, her illustrations adopted a personality similar to Antonella's – childlike, restless, and curious. She takes inspiration from TV cartoons and children's books that she used to read when she was a toddler. Antonella loves to create characters and stories to go along with them and enjoys thinking as a child, drawing like them and for them.

Made in United States
North Haven, CT
04 October 2023

42341417R00020